ANTHEA CHURCH, Head of English at Kent College Pembury in the United Kingdom, had her first novel *Fire Fly* published in 1993. She has studied and taught Raja Yoga meditation for more than 20 years, and runs courses in creativity. As a product of her deep love of silent contemplation, *Inner Beauty* published by Eternity Ink, has become one of the most enduring favourites of Raja Yoga meditation students over the past 20 years. Eternity Ink has also published her books *Inner Space, The Source* and *Angels*. *The Soul Family* was recently published by the Brazilian publishing house Editora Gente.

# INNER BEAUTY
## A BOOK OF VIRTUES

Inner Beauty
Copyright © Brahma Kumaris Australia (2024)

Published by

ETERNITY INK
181 First Avenue,
Five Dock. NSW 2046.
Australia

First edition November 1994.

Reprinted June 1996, September 2001, September 2003, June 2006, July 2008, November 2016.

This edition printed September 2024.

ISBN 978-0-9592271 54

This book has been produced on behalf of the Brahma Kumaris World Spiritual University, a non-profit organisation, with the aim to share information as a community service for the spiritual growth of individuals. The Brahma Kumaris World Spiritual University (BKWSU) exists to serve the family of humanity; to assist individuals to discover and experience their own spirituality and personal growth; to understand the significance and consequence of individual action and global interaction; and to reconnect and strengthen the eternal relationship with the supreme soul, the spiritual parent.

# Contents

Foreword 1 • Mercy 34
Accuracy 2 • Obedience 36
Benevolence 4 • Patience 39
Cheerfulness 6 • Purity 41
Cleanliness 8 • Respect 44
Contentment 10 • Self-confidence 47
Co-operation 12 • Serenity 50
Courage 15 • Simplicity 53
Detachment 17 • Stability 55
Determination 20 • Surrender 57
Discipline 22 • Sweetness 59
Flexibility 24 • Tirelessness 61
Gentleness 26 • Tolerance 63
Humility 28 • Truthfulness 65
Introversion 30 • Wisdom 67
Lightness 32 •

# FOREWORD

*V*irtue is the beauty of a person. It is what makes them lovely and unusual. It is the colour, form, shape of their personality. It is the way they do things, the way they move, speak and dress. They may have no money, but if a person has virtue, they will always seem rich, for everything that is close to them will be filled with quality. Virtue shines outward into everything, into the body, into the environment and ultimately into the fibre of the planet itself. It fills what is empty, heals what is sick, settles what is troubled. ☯ But underneath virtue must be silence, for silence is the gold that sets off the jewels and protects them from scattering. In silence a person can see how the wealth is to be spent, where to invest it and make its value grow. ☯ When silence and virtue characterise the relationship between two people, there is harmony. When silence and virtue live together in one person, there is perfection. Perfection is a possibility; otherwise there would be no word for it.

## ACCURACY

Accuracy is being in the right place at the right time; it is moving from a position of quiet to a position of speech at the right time; moving from participation to withdrawal, from work to play, from laughter to thought, from colour to plainness -- all of these at the right time. Accuracy is that most delicate point of transition from one thing to another. ☯ Accuracy gives form to all those deep feelings that fill life. It enables them to be expressed as they should be, with coherence and power. It ensures that nothing goes too far, is overdone, flogged to death. It is a gentle control, not as obvious as discipline because discipline generally inspires action whereas accuracy keeps a check on it, but is every bit as important. ☯ Accuracy comes from knowing how to live spiritually in a material world, how to make the meeting point between mind and matter a happy and precise one. An accurate person knows therefore how to retain health, because they never push themselves too far. They know to avoid weakness. They understand the most subtle effects of thought on the machinery of the body, understand the relationship between what comes into the mind and what the lips speak, between what is touched by the hands and what the actions are. Each meeting point holds a secret. Accuracy understands that. ☯ Accuracy doesn't come from forcing matter into a state of order, nor forcing yourself into quiet because you know that you shouldn't speak. It is not a panic inside which suddenly brings a blocking against expression and says, "Don't!…" It is the strength to retain depth and stillness inside so that you approach each second with respect -- slowly -- in the right way. If you move too fast, you miss the meeting point between things and become like the hare who scampered but lost the race. It is safer to be a tortoise!

# BENEVOLENCE

𝓑enevolence is silent good will. It is like the sun shining on hard ground, softening the earth, melting the ice, but with no design or intention to heal. It is a state of naturalness which is why it works because the ground feels no debt to the sun. In the same way, to be on the receiving end of benevolence is to be receiving something for which there is no return. Not even a pressure to respond - - which is why one does respond so easily. ☯ Benevolence is a state of being, reliant on itself alone. It has nothing to do with feelings of mercy or preference, sudden stabs of love; it just is. It offers nothing specific, but everyone is drawn to it. It answers no questions, but it enables you to think. It teaches nothing, but because of it you can learn. ☯ To be benevolent is to have forged a link so strong with an unbroken source of energy that even the interruptions of life cannot block that constant refuelling. However dry life is, the tide keeps turning again and again, always. And in the moments just before turning, when life has taken you to the limits, you just know that you're on the brink of a great in-flow, and so you stay quiet, acknowledging temporary emptiness - - only as a prelude. Only if you hurt someone does the tide stop turning and you are grounded and have to fight. ☯ To be benevolent is the best help you can be to anyone because benevolence has no shape, any more than sunlight has, but it can filter into the quiet corners of panic in a person's mind and lighten the burden. ☯ It is the least intrusive virtue and is welcomed everywhere.

# CHEERFULNESS

Cheerfulness is when the brow of the hill seems close. When you are taking the last few steps forward. It is the unique experience of the day before a special event, the last few moments. It is when you have passed through so much and there's only a little to go, and that little is easy, because you'd only lose if you turned back. Cheerfulness is the brilliance of being free, even of having to choose, because everything you've done up to this point has already dictated the future. So how can we be cheerful, when we've got so far to go? ❧ It is a matter of clarity and conviction. First you have to be able to see beyond the present, to have such vision that you can sense a good future, not just for you, but for everything. You have to know in your bones that the whole movement of life is towards what is good and that all hills have valleys, all seasons have summer. Then you have to live that or else cheerfulness is just bravado in the face of despair. ❧ Cheerfulness in its true form is earned. You have to work for it, clear away enough of the rubbish inside that you can see. For this you have to know how to cordon off weakness, to refuse it entry into the rest of your life. People talk about being "whole" but, until the end, you have to become an expert at being in pieces, so that your eyes are always dancing even if your feet are dragging. ☯ Cheerfulness is never being ashamed, any more than you would be by getting paint on your hands as you fill in the last few brush strokes. Cheerfulness makes everyone love you, because they can sense your victory ahead, but it is not a cold victory -- alone -- as the foothold for others to follow is the mud on your boots.

# CLEANLINESS

*C*leanliness of spirit means coming close, without fear; to accept a penetrating gaze knowing you've nothing to hide. It comes with a happy mind and constant checking. Happiness in the mind is based on serenity. Not reacting suddenly to mood or circumstance, neither flinching at adversity nor jumping for joy. A pliancy in which the spirit just moves with the times, quiet but alert. Cleanliness is also based on fulfilment of the senses. When the eyes are seeing the unseen and the ears hearing the unheard, piercing the subtleties of life, there is happiness. When reactions are based not on the incoming messages, on what is second hand, but on the deep original knowledge that is first hand, there is happiness. There is happiness when the mind meets life freshly, doesn't fall into patterns or expect too much, but recognises its own value simply because it is a marvellous piece of machinery. There is happiness when the mind is nurtured. This nurturing is a constant checking, a vigilance, against impostors. When a mind is working deeply, it is alert, but sometimes in its silence it misses the superficial threats, the endless flow of thoughts from other minds to which it is exposed constantly. The mind can imagine these thoughts are its own and instead of straightforwardly expelling them, it tries to train them into quietness. This is called working with dirt. Anything that lands on the mind from outside and slips into its reactions is a pollution of the spirit. To be alert to the challenge is called life. ☯ So what is cleanliness? It is maintaining absolutely who you are, reacting from the core of you, disentangling irrelevance, moving forward in a straight line. And if anyone scrutinises the person, they see only honest hard work which doesn't mind being watched, because it knows that perfection is on the horizon. A way off, but there.

# CONTENTMENT

Contentment is like an underground river whose course just cannot be daunted. On the surface, people are stamping, pushing, pulling; the ground is cracking or left derelict but underneath, the river is flowing; even if at some point it is only a trickle in the darkness.  ❧  Water on ground level is always at risk of pollution or being dried up, used, drunk, drawn on, but subterranean water is untapped. Contentment is the same. It is a constant unseen movement forward. Not oblivious of challenge, but when the landscape of the mind, the surface of life, undergoes some upheaval the river responds, changes, flows in and around, even though still unseen. It just never dries up.  ❧  A profound understanding is needed for someone to be content -- a need to know and gently anticipate the movements of the mind and also to feel the pull of the destination that lies beyond everything. Contentment is a study of life, not just a bland acceptance of it. People say not to think too much but, to be content, you have to enjoy thinking very deeply, watching very carefully, responding very quietly, moving with the times. And more than anything, the river needs the force of the current to move through the strange humps and bumps of the subconscious. Without the current, there can be intelligence, but there will always be depression, a feeling that you may just get stuck. ☯ The current is spiritual force.

## CO-OPERATION

Co-operation is perhaps one of the least recognised but most valuable of human virtues. It isn't recognised because it is not part of an end product. It is to do with the process of achieving something and thus its greatness lies in the fact that it is expressed through ordinary everyday actions. ☯ A person who has this virtue is a little like the sun shining down on an outdoor event in a place where it normally rains. The event is praised, but afterwards the sun is forgotten. The analogy works, not because there is any virtue in the weather (on the contrary) but because it demonstrates how vital and yet undistinguished co-operation is. Without it the event is dead. ☯ So, for a person to be co-operative means for them to have a quiet eye for what is needed to bring success, and to supply it (and no more) at the right time, in the right place and then to be off. Someone who co-operates, offers their services and then splashes their name on the achievement is not co-operative. It requires invisibility and precision to do and then to go without waiting for results. It also takes a discerning eye to see exactly what is needed, to be removed sufficiently from your own approach to a task and just to contribute one ingredient. Sometimes not even an idea, but however clever you may consider yourself to be, just a hand, a support. ☯ Now, to an extent, almost everyone expresses this virtue. Everyone will co-operate in something that they care about. But actually to have this virtue "full time" means to be constantly extending your hand wherever it is needed. And, even if there is nothing visible to be done, the world still needs the support of tranquil minds. ☯ Underlying this virtue, therefore, is something which isn't the least ordinary: a profound optimism about the future of life in general. If co-operation occurs only in conjunction with individual tasks, that is nothing, but if it springs from the understanding that every act of generosity is contributing to a whole new creation, then it becomes something great. It is fuel for a new world, as is every human virtue when consciously based on a vision of the future. Perhaps this is what is meant by the term "being at one with the world": when everything you do is thrown into the pool, rather than being a personal move in a personal game. ☯ So what is this vision of the "new creation"? Clearly it has not a lot to do with God creating bodies and a land of milk and honey. No. It is only the creation of virtue in human minds. A very intricate process with a great deal of opposition but, say one word, have one thought, do one thing to uplift another human mind and you have already contributed to it in a significant way.

# Courage

*C*ourage thinks only of the destination and nothing in between. It is the force of a decided will behind every move and so failure is far from it. Courage is when you can't necessarily see, but in your heart you know and that knowing becomes a light to see by, so you do not stop. Courage grows with life, but it is also the quality of a child who knows no challenge and of an adult who is ignorant of the challenge's power. ☯ Courage is to take a step forward into an area of difficulty without a solution in mind, and yet feeling that victory is ahead. It is going empty-handed, but knowing that God's hand is stretched out to pull you. ☯ Courage is saying what you believe, undiluted, desiring no approval, knowing that a deeply thought-out ideal is strong enough to withstand opposition. And if it is knocked down, then courage knows not to blame, but to rebuild more strongly. ☯ Courage doesn't come unbidden, merely in a moment of danger. It is the fruit of consistent effort to play life by the rules. Its expression is the tip of something enormous, formed over years. A rock below the surface which, just visible, becomes an island for others to rest on. You know when courage is there in someone. You can sense it and it makes you trust them. ☯ There is something touching about a courageous person too, because "all the odds seem against them", but you know they'll make it, for they have the strength of quality with them against the weakness of quantity. They say less and do more and they never make promises for the courage in them knows that, together with a high aim, there has to be an intelligent mind that is able to move quietly, one step at a time. Courage is boldness, but it is always careful.

# DETACHMENT

Many spiritual paths advocate a mental state called detachment, in which a person moves away from worldly concerns and becomes an observer of life. This is considered to be a means of reaching an inner goal, because it frees you from distractions and conflict. Raja Yoga also teaches "detachment", but the image used to explain the concept is not that of a dusty-footed pilgrim, scaling a mountain, but a lotus-flower.

The main thing about a lotus-flower is that it has its roots in the mud. It cannot grow without the mud and yet its petals are pristine. This is detachment. Detachment is being close to what you most want to be free of and using it to make you grow. Not separating yourself from anything. Take your own personality. Usually there are aspects of yourself which, either you are unaware of, or you just don't like. Unconscious, you distort them into something attractive. Hence hard work in a person often denotes fear of disapproval. This is the direct opposite of detachment: doing something, not for its own value, but to enhance your personal position. ☯ The lotus-flower doesn't turn mud into anything. Mud is mud. Yet the mud has nutrients needed to aid the flower's growth.

It is the same for us. We are in a situation that we don't like -- "in the mud". And yet it is probably the most secure position there is if we could only recognise it, not distort it, and let it "grow" us. Or alternatively, we want to be free of someone, to be alone, but the relationship has somehow caught hold of us. The person now close to us is probably the best teacher we could have, if we were only able to see the "nutrient" in their presence; if we could recognise, too, that we are probably focusing on a very minor aspect of their personality, and totally disregarding the rest. Detachment is freedom from slants and bias of this kind. It means seeing the whole picture. Or again, we have made a mess of something, exposed ourselves to criticism, usually upsetting, until there is the ability to be detached from the task at which we have failed, to stop possessing it and just appreciate its inherent value and recognise that it will get done anyway. Painting for painting's sake, for the beauty of painting, not for the beauty of "my" painting. And painting, certainly, will always continue, quite regardless of me. ☯ So, detachment means standing right next to our enemies and responding to them with sincerity and effort and seeing how suddenly they disappear, like wild animals sloping off gently in the face of fearlessness and peace. On the other hand, detachment also means not touching, moving right away so that you can see a thing properly. Being an emotional weather*person*, being able to gauge and predict and prepare. Detachment is to be free of time, and most importantly to be free of the distorting perspective which places "I" at the centre of the universe. In small ways, this consciousness helps a lot. You begin to realise that when someone talks to you, you are not necessarily the focus of their attention, but that they are bringing with them a hundred other thoughts and concerns, You are only a foothold on their way. ☯ Detachment is a very great virtue. It brings emotional safety, realism and refreshment. It makes others feel free with you, free to come and go without a fuss. But the moment you stop loving life, then detachment becomes impossible, because you begin to hold on to things that help. ☯ Detachment is best learnt from God, who sees everything but never stops loving. It is best demonstrated by the lotus-flower which touches mud, touches rock-bottom but never loses its beauty. Beauty means to keep growing -- always.

## DETERMINATION

𝒟etermination is an unbroken line, a backbone. It is when every situation is anchored to an unseen aim that keeps everything together. Without determination, life becomes scattered. Experiences are pleasant and kept, unpleasant and left. When life is random and one is at the mercy of life. ❧ Determination makes you sit up straight and love everything, because it's all part of moving forward. Day and night you have the feeling that you only have to seek and you can touch the hard core of wisdom that rests inside each moment. You can focus on that, let the toughness be in seeking that and then action is automatically as it should be. Gently right. ❧ Battering at life from the outside, trying to change what's visible is inverted determination. It makes your face hard and unyielding and though it may bring visible success, there can be a floundering inside. Determination is not, therefore, a matter so much of action as of stillness. When a quality of mind -- peace, happiness, depth, purity -- can remain still and uninterrupted by the bumps of life, that is true determination. Such stability, maintained for long enough, penetrates the surface of life anyway and it changes. The bumps go. ❧

You have to feed determination, to nourish the qualities you wish to keep with you constantly. How? By understanding them, examining them, using them. They are a part of your nature anyway, but it's been winter for so long that they've gone underground. Sometimes you have to burrow to find them and coax them to the surface. Hence the need for silence. ☯ Silence brings the strength to go on, the steadiness to succeed, the softness to slip past difficulties unnoticed. If determination breaks, it's best to stop for a few moments, be silent and find value again, or else what you do will be spineless. Feel the bones of the situation, then fall in love with the task.

# DISCIPLINE

*D*iscipline comes from inside. If it is imposed or assumed for show, it is like putting on a coat. You wear it outside where it is seen but, come inside where it is hot, you just take it off. In the privacy of your own problems it just becomes a burden; you want to be free of it. Real discipline is part of you. It is an expression of respect for life which is why you put the coat on in the first place; but it is also an expression of respect for yourself, which is why you keep it on -- even when things are hard. ☯ In fact it is natural to be disciplined, to follow a pattern of existence that has order. Nature has order. Happiness and sorrow, though sometimes not understood, have their set time. Nothing is naturally random. Even death is at the mercy of a system. We just can't see it. So there is an attraction to discipline, which is why real freedom isn't always what it appears to be and which is why we eventually get unhappy when we do not embrace a routine. ☯ Discipline requires a tangible goal, an adoption of something larger than yourself which is guiding your attitude; otherwise, how do you know what's wrong, what to strive for? Nothing is wrong unless you have the mirror of a system to look into. It may just be the system of a profession or the channelling of a talent. A dancer just wouldn't wear four inch heels; an athlete wouldn't, either, and a politician would watch his words. At best though, it comes from something beyond these, something spiritual which outlives either talent or profession. When discipline comes from a commitment of the spirit, it brings unbroken safety. It sets off the fire of love with a kind of coolness. It keeps you in the middle of the road. No sudden standstills before the journey is over. In sickness there is safety, because discipline makes you sustain precision when it would be easier just to let go; in happiness there is safety, because discipline stops you spilling too much feeling for others to slip on; in sorrow there is safety because discipline makes you go on walking through the actions which will bring back your joy. In all moods, discipline gently holds you steady. Discipline is mercy. It becomes a voice inside which softens the resistance of weakness and ushers you towards freedom.

# FLEXIBILITY

Flexibility is the beauty of a child whose bones have not yet been hardened, whose body has not yet begun to store the effects, the tensions of life. Instead, there is smoothness, quickness, joy. Flexibility in an adult is not suppleness of body, but subtlety of thought, such vigilance that there is no storing or harbouring of pain. It is pain that causes blockages, stops ease of response and cuts happiness dead. It is rare to find a flexible adult, one who hasn't become a "walking habit" but who is still reacting freshly, unconditioned, unafraid. How is it possible? ❧ One secret is renewal. If there is a constant flow of new feelings, it is like a shower washing away the bits and pieces of reactions unexpressed which, if left, accumulate to form fears or prejudices. To find new feelings, to refuel, you don't have to go anywhere, except inside you, away from the obvious. Going away from the obvious is a spiritual holiday, and a person is always easier when they've been away. ❧ The problem with normal holidays is that you cannot bring the sunshine back with you. To be flexible you have to go away, mentally withdraw, but you also have to return bearing something deep and original from inside, something to use, or else the shock of bumping into life again makes you start and harden. ☯ Withdrawing is a habit, should be sacredly held, as should rising early or eating in peace. These are the doors that you can stumble through if in trouble and find composure again. So, whilst child-likeness, softness, is the beauty of being flexible, discipline is its basis. ☯ But you can be too strict. When habits have been adopted as systems and you can't get rid of them, when they haven't been internalised and deeply appreciated, then life is rigid and dull. Where there is flexibility, you can let go of everything visible, because the discipline is part of your bones. ☯ In a perfect world, flexibility would simply be an expression of joy, an unbidden somersault into the air, suppleness of mind and body together. A dance. In the meantime, flexibility means moving with the times, slipping through life as gently and strongly as possible. And above all, making all problems into teachers.

# GENTLENESS

*I*f trees had souls, perhaps the quality most attributable to them would be gentleness. Gentleness is not a lack of strength but a quality which doesn't disturb, doesn't push, yet knows its power and can provide shelter. ❧ Trees. Enormous structures capable of destroying within seconds, with massively complex systems of growth and decay. No wonder humanity has picked the image of the tree to illustrate its own history: the tree of life. And yet, so simple, so gentle. Wherever the seed falls, regardless of atmosphere, of even often suitability, it just grows, stopped by nothing except human violence. And it never tries to be anything other than what it is, which is the tendency that most disturbs. Oaks won't suddenly lose their 'oakness', unless cross-pollinated or something equally unnatural. Nor does it hurt. Though towering over an animal or insignificant tangle of bushes, a tree won't touch. In fact, it provides shelter. ❧ As far as we know, trees don't have souls. But there are souls who are like trees, enormous in their thinking and yet totally gentle. This isn't the gentleness of insecurity. That can fool sometimes. I remember a girl at my school like who was very clever, and yet her writing lacked rigour and her poems were always perfect until the last line, where the rhyme was wrong. It seemed to be her gentleness that was keeping her just a touch off brilliance. But now, I think she was just afraid or didn't know how good she was. Real gentleness in a person is a great power. The power that sees, understands but never interferes. Like the branch of the tree, just touching the earth but never taking root in it. Never to take root in someone else's mind but to help, that's gentleness.

☯ It is hard not to refer to God when thinking of these things. Imagine the being in the universe who sees and understands everything and yet the one who remains completely apart, approaching only on invitation. A relationship with God is an ideal one, because life is dramatically influenced and yet only as it would be by standing next to someone completely still, who was just teaching you how to look. Not saying: look at me, I'll show you, but just: be here and you'll see how to work on your life. We all need that gentle tree to sit under.

# Humility

$\mathcal{H}$umility dismisses nothing, but takes even small things seriously. It is the recognition that whatever is in life and is in front of you is to be respected as something that will take you forward; that inside big things there is sometimes little, but inside little there is often enormity. ☯ Humility puts a hand out to nothing extra, but simply takes what's there. Whether that be food or clothing or understanding. Sometimes there is a lot available and sometimes only little. It doesn't matter. Even when you understand nothing, there is no worry, for in humility there is the trust that if a person feels themselves to be a child of God, everything will come anyway, at the right time. And knowledge mistimed is as dangerous as ignorance. ☯ Humility is also a basis on which things happen: a carefulness and simple being to create from. For in it there is no expectation of brilliance and therefore accomplishment comes more naturally, unthreatened by what will be said or thought by others. A humble person is lovely to be with, for beside them one is at one's best. Yet, because they respect themselves, nothing done belittles them, but further speaks of their beauty because the achievement is half theirs already. ☯ Every creative task needs humility behind it, for humility is plainness and on plainness the colours and shape of the work are clear to see and mould. If a new world were to come, it would need this quiet basis to form itself on, that could stay the same whilst things were changing. ☯ Humility is special, therefore, and yet, at times, its disguise it so ordinary. For when something valuable is forming, ordinariness and noise are sometimes needed to distract attention as it grows. The humility in a person, carefree of reputation, can wear the disguise easily so that nothing of the real work is seen. ☯ Humility is the willingness to be used in any way that's necessary, however out of character it may seem; for, in humility, individuality has been exchanged for the task it is involved in. Quietness in this case, is an unquestioning acceptance of whatever has to be done. ☯ Humility is rare because to have it, you have to want nothing. If you do have it, you get everything.

# INTROVERSION

*I*ntroversion is the meeting point between beauty and plainness. It is when on the outside there are only love and warmth, the qualities of any decent human life, but on the inside there are wisdom and perception. It is when on the outside there are relationships with a few, and on the inside there is enough to fuel a relationship with the world; on the outside there is concern for the present and on the inside there is awareness of the future. Introversion is the door which divides the two, not exclusively, because a door will always open, but protectively because it is night and there are thieves about. ☯ What is night? Night is when no-one really knows what they want or what they are doing. Night is when people question things; so, the door has to be locked because, when people don't know what they want, they steal anything. The treasures of a mind, developing in silence, are always at risk. So there has to be enforced caution. ☯ Introversion should also be exercised after a party where there has been a sharing of valuables. Here, it has gently to close the door to even the closest friends and then invite solitude. It is the caution which checks carefully whom it invites in, in the first place, not out of fear but out of love for what has been given in trust to take care of. ☯ And yet introversion is not silence any more than real solitude is. ☯ It is participation, but not only participation. It is speaking with peace, walking with humility, working with love. When action is accompanied by a depth of quality, this is a sign of introversion. It is when instead of staying within, you choose to venture through the door, taking with you something of value to all. ☯ It won't always be night. A time will come when morning will arrive. What happens then? The curtains are drawn and what's inside is visible through the windows. The eyes reflect clearly the life of the mind. Still it can't be touched, but it can be seen and enjoyed. ☯ And when day comes, windows and doors are flung open. The mind is open, accessible and the sunlight makes equal what's inside with what's outside. That will be a time where privacy and "individuality", protection and caution will have passed. A unique period of sharing, when minds will be so light that they can pass through each other unhurt. A time when the virtue that introversion has protected will be poured into a common source of joy. It will be heaven.

# LIGHTNESS

*L*ightness is like hitting a spring of water inside. A sudden break-out from the dryness of your normal reactions as you begin to express from within, rather than just responding to what you see outside. It usually happens when you come upon a quality that hasn't been destroyed or jaded by time, something very old and inherent in you that has survived birth after birth. Most qualities and talents are developed through use, but are also in some way diluted and changed. Lightness is touching what makes you unique because it has never changed. ☯ What happens then? Laughter. Laughter bubbles out into your life. It may be that you've touched gentleness, eternal, unchanged gentleness, but the spring seems always to come out in laughter. And the charm and joy of the laughter protects the gentleness that you've found because someone who is laughing touches everyone, but cannot be touched. ☯ And as the laughter strengthens, two things happen. First comes the tendency to touch the value in others because innocence reaches the part in people that society teaches them to hide. Secondly, the quality inside grows. The spring becomes a river and starts to flow through life in a more open, forceful way. So, from a deep, private discovery, it becomes a part of your living. Not only that, it becomes a resource for others. You can just sit beside a river and without it doing anything, you get in touch with how you really are and where you are going. Perhaps that was what the scriptures meant when they told the story of Siddhartha.

## MERCY

Mercy is the quality that sees behind expression to the need that is inside it. Behind the anger to the sadness, behind the coldness to the fear. Mercy goes behind and meets the hidden needs of a person's mind, their child-self. To have mercy is to know the vulnerability that is in you and feed it with what you are learning, so that it strengthens and becomes level with your adulthood and calmness. Mercy is to know that though it asks for what is visible and material, often the mind's needs are deeper and more demanding and cannot be met by anything false or short-term. Mercy is the wisdom to see that a failing mind needs a system in which to meet its needs. Real mercy is not, therefore, merely softness or compassion, but a spiritual system whose clear footsteps hold God's presence and so, followed, become a meeting point with him. That meeting is itself the most valuable present a human mind can receive. In it lies a training for the senses, a training to draw them inward so that, alone from influence, the mind can regain its strength and learn what is unique to it -- as though, in a moment of quiet victory, it receives its own inheritance. When a mind finds its strength again, it develops the confidence to re-enter the world and be alive and gifted in it. Mercy is to keep the strictness until the last moment and to help others do the same, so that they no longer bank their lives on temporary attractions, but move towards the hidden beauty that is in them. ☯ This is why it is wrong to blame someone, for blame sees only what is outside and not what lies behind it. Mercy is to think, do and speak only what leads inward to where the real reasons "lie".

## OBEDIENCE

$\mathcal{O}$bedience brings stillness. Not the stillness of no movement, but the stillness of everything moving in the right direction naturally. It is like the tide pulled by the moon to turn. There may be all kinds of movement and unrest in the water but the tide will always turn because of the moon. ☯ Obedience is when the rebellions of the mind turn back on themselves like waves and retreat because of the strength of spirituality moving them. It is not force, but the creation of a natural rhythm. From noise into quiet, questioning into silence. ☯ Where there is disobedience within oneself, there is great danger. There is the danger of an ocean breaking through a wall, drowning within one go the careful creation of thought, whole homes and families of ideas gone. There is the danger of impulse and dreams. There is so much danger. ☯ The story of the tide turning is absolutely precise. Look at a chart and you know when it is safe to set sail. An obedient mind can be relied on in the same way. It is not boring to be obedient to oneself -- it is the landing strip for the most challenging of flights. Keep to the rules and you are totally free. You are trusted and beautiful. It is very rare to find someone with an obedient mind. ☯ Steps towards obedience are the steps of a dance. They move in stages. The first step is practised alone. A constant attention to one movement over and over again. This is the obedience of the mind. The rhythmic retreat and advance of troubled thinking. You start to think, extend, and then, with gentle precision, withdraw the thought, before it hurts. The withdrawing isn't a sign that there is something wrong. It is part of the step. ☯ The second stage is learning the dance, putting the steps together. That starts with bowing to the teacher, accepting something or someone to learn from. Obedience is following the dance of the teacher, practising alone and then watching, with intensity and exhilaration, as the steps become a dance. ☯ The first two stages demand no more than attention and dedication. ☯ The last step takes courage. This is obedience to circumstance. And this is when the slow, private dance of love becomes public. To be still inside, to be obedient to your own principles is one thing; to follow the teacher, silently harmonising, is also one thing, but to be obedient to circumstance is another. ☯ This is when the world is blaring, demanding, impinging and yet you maintain your rhythm, maintain precision, keep dancing, but not in a vacuum. You give to life. Instead of inner discipline being a withdrawal, it becomes a source of pleasure. Ultimate obedience is when you've learnt the steps, you know the dance and however unmusical the situation, whatever the danger of collision and hurt, you invite others to dance with you. Not just invite, but the dance of obedience becomes your religion.

## PATIENCE

*O*ne of the principal aims of all spiritual people is to eradicate the barriers. Yet patience is the creation of a barrier: a gentle but implacable barrier, dividing feeling from expression. It is not a dead barrier, a brick wall, but something live, built systematically over a long space of time. It is also a protection. ☯ On one side, there is feeling. Feelings run deep and fast. They would flood life, given half a chance. Swim along with them and whilst there can be exhilaration, there can also be drowning. Without any barrier, feeling finds instant expression. Life is simply a series of actions done with spontaneity and words are the same. ☯ For someone with any sense of beauty and control, there has to be patience in between. Patience doesn't do anything, any more than a wall does, it simply slows you down. Slowing down expression is the first way to speed up spiritual progress. It also, unlike a wall, opens up your vision, gives you time to assess the future: gently, to think. ☯ One of the forces most challenging to patience is not other people, but simply one's own body. Watch to what extent verbal expression is dictated by the state of the body: the body feels heavy, the mind feels heavy and the words fall like lead on the air; the body is well and life follows suit. ☯ Patience lets ill health bounce off it. It comes in between, does nothing, just is, like the wall, or the traditional form of the protective mother whose very presence offers refuge. And just as a child can sit on a mother's lap, so, too, you can sit on the "wall" of patience and just watch. It is often dangerous to do anything else. ☯ Sometimes patience makes you persist, to go on with something you'd rather see finished. The wall, ever still, turns its back on feeling and simply faces the future. Keep going. Keep going. If a mother stopped helping a child to walk, we'd still all be crawling. And sometimes we are, in our minds. So patience is a wonderful measure against indiscretion but it is also a means of encouragement. ☯ Means and measures are temporary. One day the wall will be knocked down. When feelings have grown up sufficiently to be worthy of instant expression, that will be the moment of freedom. For anyone pursuing the life of spirituality, it is a natural aim; to become whole, no drill-sergeants or self-criticism, not even patience, just joy.

## PURITY

$\mathcal{L}$ike the word "virtue", "purity" is a word, in the West certainly, which is associated with religious movements, advocating total abstinence from pleasure. It is often regarded with some amusement, even scorn, and yet, in fact, it is the basis for the greatest human accomplishment. It is the foundation of virtue. How? ❦ Imagine a really beautiful room, perfectly, if simply furnished, flooded with natural sunlight, soft pastel-washed walls, thick carpets, ornaments positioned with precision but ease. Someone walks in, sits down, picks something up, puts it down in a different place, stands up, leaving cushions dipped and creased. A second person enters, puts on some music, starts a conversation. Then a third, a fourth, a fifth. The volume increases. An argument begins. It's meant to be a party. Then suddenly, something is broken. Something very precious. With the noise, the hostess, anxious, worn but with a sense of quality about her, walks in. But it is too late. Her lack of vigilance has taken its toll. ❦ This is the story of purity. All human beings have a space inside which is filled with virtue, with possessions and treasures. For some, the space may be small, for others there is a neglected palace somewhere in their souls. When a soul begins its life, that space is completely unspoilt, filled with light. But when the first person walks in, when a person allows that sanctuary to be invaded, something is lost. It may just be a dip in their integrity, but something has gone. They have stretched out their hand, perhaps initially as a gesture of friendship, but with this gesture has come the force of external influence and the inroad into self-esteem. ☯ One person has entered, then a second, a third, a fourth. A party. Each visitor comes with an idea and the noise of disagreement begins. Humanity is now abuzz with internal rowdy parties. Then, the breakage. This comes for all of us, though, if the noise is loud enough, we may not even notice the moment when the most personal and valued aspect of our being is smashed. The worst point: when our talents -- whatever they may be -- are destroyed. ☯ At that point, we just have to stop and meditate, to call an end to the party completely. Every hostess knows it takes supreme strength to stop and clear up after a party. Much easier to go to sleep and do it later. What is needed? Internally, an invitation to a supreme strength to come and restore light and order. God. A truly pure soul can walk right through you leaving no mark at all, only a sense of light and optimism. As they leave you, you feel that you are genuinely alone again, alone to appreciate the special quality within you that their presence has so gently highlighted. When God walks into your life, it is like a laser beam passing across your being. The mess is horribly visible. And yet as the light enters, its principal tendency is to restore beauty and value. Meditation is an invitation to light. So, what does God say about purity? God doesn't say to be alone, to hide from the world, to be like a fastidious housewife who winces when anything is touched. God enjoys a party, but he teaches respect, the respect which enjoys company, conversation, laughter, but allows no lasting impression to be made on one's mental environment.

# RESPECT

*R*espect is never catching anyone out, never pulling at their shortcomings so that they become a target for laughter. It means watching and nurturing strength and it is based on the awareness that everyone has value because everyone is unique. It rests also on humility, because humility knows that what's visible in a fool is only a chapter of their whole story. ❧ So, respect is keeping yourself equidistant between strength and weakness. Not advertising strength outright but gently highlighting it, by giving it a task. With a child, it is not saying: you're such a good painter, but just giving it paper and brushes; with a child, not saying: you're a hopeless painter, but just giving it paper and a pen instead. Never to ignore weakness for that is disrespect, just to provide a different focus. ❧ Where there is real respect there is the understanding that talents are constantly changing and sometimes what is seen is just a matter of where the light is falling. Where the sun isn't shining doesn't indicate a gap; only that something is resting in the shadow. You just never know what's there, so it's best not to kill anyone by categorising them. ❧ Respect is very cooling, because it values space, knows that though love brings the balance, everyone needs time, a pause, a chance to breathe quietly, alone. It stops you going too close too quickly, and it lets people grow in their own time. Respect never urges and only strikes where there's the strength to withstand. ☯ It is as fruitful to respect things as it is to respect people. To respect things has its origin in respecting the body, with all its strengths and weaknesses. To approach with the same balance, neither selling beauty nor ridiculing ugliness, neither advertising health nor indulging pain. The middle way is like standing in the doorway, touching nothing. It means you can leave easily. ☯ Where there has been disregard for anyone or anything, there is hurt. The repercussions are enormous. Where a person has been hurt, the rebound is often obscure and dangerous, hard to identify, because you can't just say: you've hurt me. It's hard to be direct; so, someone walking by suddenly gets hit instead and a whole chain begins. Where a thing has been abused, disrespected, then it causes trouble. It breaks, makes a mess, holds you up. Either way, disrespect takes away freedom and blocks the way. ☯ Where there is respect, it is like forging a straight path through life, so that you can reach a point of stillness and then, looking back, see only light. Nothing pushed into the shadows, either, to create short cuts and so, no sudden reawakenings of old feelings. You've walked poised through life, observing the ups and downs with dignity. The result is that the respect you've given returns to you -- a rebound.

# SELF-CONFIDENCE

𝒮elf-confidence is knowing your way around yourself, knowing the ins and outs so instinctively that you always have a strength to draw on. ☯ Somewhere inside, from the stillness, you can find something. Even areas of weakness don't shake the mind, because they're already under demolition. They're empty houses that your thoughts don't even bother to enter any more. And if you do bump into such a part of you, confidence brings the power to walk gently away. Where there is no confidence, you think you ought to stay and make a display of what is bad, a celebration of the weak. ☯ Self-confidence makes you move more slowly, speak more quietly, stop to look at whom you're communicating with instead of flattening life by rushing heavily on. It enables you to stand happily and quietly in a gap of ignorance and let everyone wait until you're ready. Then in the quietness, to fill the moment with strength before a word has been said. And when nerves persist in shaking your poise, it enables you to administer softness and silence and make the whole machine calm down. Self-confidence runs deeper, much deeper than nerves. ☯ Self-confidence works gently, but it can also cut sharply the web of false connections that make you think that people are criticising. And at its strongest, it makes it possible to disintegrate a thought in someone's mind before it's even been realised by the thinker. So they were going to shoot, but they veer off into passivity. Confidence is power. ☯ What is the method to gain self-confidence? One way is to talk, not to others but to yourself, At moments of insecurity, it's warming to talk to someone else, but it is safe to talk to yourself because inside there is a reserve of love that will see you through anything. Friendship isn't so consistent or eternal. After talking to yourself, giving nerves a niche to quietly panic in, then it's best to "do". Action, together with quiet love, kills nerves and creates a reserve of courage that, stored, can be drawn on later. The more you love, then do, the deeper the store of coinage, and the less you have to prime yourself. Ultimately the love you needed can be given to someone else. Complete and untouched. And not only love: peace, serenity, loyalty... can all be given, without you touching them. Life may be asking you to be determined, but you can still find a drop of serenity for someone else's use. Then you're not just giving, on the basis of mood, but you're filling a need. ☯ Where confidence is deep, there is the foundation for real giving. Real means "I" am silent, no jangling nerves or loud thoughts, Stillness. And in that stillness, I can hear you.

# SERENITY

$\mathcal{S}$erenity is depth. It is when the energy of thought, so often dissipated by expression through the senses, is directed deep within the mind. It is when seeing with the eyes stops and seeing with the mind's eye begins; it is when hearing with the ears stops and hearing with the inner ear begins; it is when speaking with the mouth stops and communication through thought begins; it is when touching with the hands stops and touching with feelings begins. Serenity is living under water but riding with joy on the surface. No serenity is existing with a struggle on the surface and never touching the depths. ☯ Why is serenity important? Because the experience of life through the senses is one of tremendous instability. The messages brought to me from life above the water, are changing constantly and at great speed. Sometimes I am exposed to pleasure but, as often, to pain. And sometimes the messages are conflicting. There is no system in the world, no fixed dose of good or bad experience. I'll just never quite know what the day holds. ☯ The experience of life "under water" is quite different. It is an experience which has its own form completely and can be utterly distinct from what life appears to be offering. And yet the deep pleasure gained from living it can nourish my response to everything that does happen on the surface. Not in any obvious way. If I've discovered a sudden understanding of love, I'm not going to splash it on my life, but it will bring a natural quietness and depth to my day. ☯ As with all virtues, there is a superficial form of serenity and a real form. Faces can have a kind of bland serenity, an expression of stillness and a certain beauty and, we say, "What a serene face she has!" But this can just denote an absence of deep thought. The real sign of serenity is not to be seen so much on the face as in the eyes. The smoothness of faces is constantly under threat but eyes say everything. In fact, one of the better proofs of serenity is when the face is emotionally weather-beaten, but the eyes retain depth and stillness. No-one can avoid being tossed about by life, but to be "tossed" and yet still be able to "dive" and touch your own strength, this shows only in the eyes. When a stone is thrown into such a person's life -- a criticism, a problem, a challenge -- only the surface is rippled. Nothing more. Even throw a knife and the impact is quite quickly absorbed, the water calm again. ☯ There is only one threat to someone with this virtue. Pollution. Pollution is when an atmosphere penetrates the surface of the water and robs the depths of their clarity. This can happen when someone impresses me. It is not that I am attracted to them so much through the senses, but their thought and ideas move me inside and gently I accept their presence in the deeper part of my being, which should remain sacred. It is not wrong to enjoy the ideas of others. In fact it is good. But there must be enough self-respect to say No to endless interruptions; otherwise, together with the pleasure of playing with someone else's thoughts, I will also begin to sustain their conflicts. Suddenly they become my conflicts too. ☯ There is only one atmosphere that I invoke with great joy into my underwater self and that is the atmosphere of God's being because God's main characteristics are constancy and lightness. He does not seek to change me, only to reinforce me and give strength to my solitude. It is quite an odd thing that the most powerful being in the universe is also the being who is the least intrusive. He doesn't interfere. In fact he is the guardian of my serenity.

## SIMPLICITY

There was once a man called Kasper Hauser. Brought up in a German prison, in the 17th century, completely unschooled in even the most basic skills of human communication, he was released at the age of about thirty and placed like an exhibit in the centre of a village square with a letter in his hand written by the prison warder, and left. The letter gave information about Hauser's upbringing and invited any willing family to take him in. ☯ Kasper Hauser looked like an animal, grunted like an animal, ate like an animal and was greeted by the villagers as an animal. Ten years later he was acclaimed a national hero. Why? Because from beneath the inarticulate speech and barbarity, there emerged a profound clarity of mind which floored many of the 17th century German academics and philosophers. He could answer questions that they could not. He was a scholar of life but he also had the virtue of simplicity. ☯ Without advocating barbaric conditions or animalism, there does seem to be a lesson here. Kasper Hauser had been forced by circumstance to limit his physical needs totally and, because isolated, was oblivious of public opinion. Because of this his natural wisdom could come to the surface. ☯

Meditation also has the same effect. By teaching yourself to be free of unnecessary clutter, by developing a love for internal solitude, two things happen. First your lifestyle takes on a simplicity and easiness that, in itself, can be a healing source to those around you; and secondly, your powers of perception become dramatically heightened. It really is like being able to see again. Occasionally there is a challenge: Why have you given everything up? But the feeling is that only negativity has been given up. The wealth of experiences accumulated over the past has not been rejected, only the pain. Someone holding onto pain can never be simple.

☯ But it is a great paradox that simplicity comes from passing through many stages of learning. It is a complex landscape before reaching a calm, straight, simple sea. It is the virtue of the spiritually old and yet also it is the possession of the physically young. ☯ And perhaps most touching of all, it belongs to God, who holds within his understanding the ups and downs of the entire human landscape. Listening to God's words is like listening to someone playing a scale on the piano when he could play a concerto. Just a scale, but done perfectly. This is simplicity.

## STABILITY

*S*tability is love of equanimity in the midst of adventure. It is the straight flat runway which allows the plane to take off to a new way of seeing things. No hasty departures, dramatic exits, but a gentle, strong take-off to brilliance. Everything packed, understood, stored, but nothing dangling carelessly, to be pulled at by questioning fingers. ☯ It is very easy and pleasant to fly flags on earth but it stops you flying inside. To say thanks to praise and pin it to your lapel just weighs you down. Try and be free then and you can't. You're too noticed to leave. Equanimity has gone. ☯ To be stable takes immense alertness, to watch the approach of praise, catch it and divert it to God, where it's due. And if there's a single thing missing inside, then when it's offered, you take it, thinking it will fit the gap, but it doesn't and then you're lumbered with it. ☯ An equally great challenge to stability is insult. When you're doing your best and someone pushes you and it's the last straw, you topple; when you're not doing your best, it's worse. And the deeper the stability, the more subtle and searching the challenges that come. They're like hailstones chipping away at your heart. Stability at its deepest is flying free of everything, resting quiet above praise, but it is also having two feet firmly on the ground, so that you can't be charged with negligence because that's an obvious target. ☯ Above all, stability comes from understanding that, whilst you should remain level-headed, life is full of ups and downs. When praise is in the air, you've got to be in the air too, free, light, empty, above, and then return, ready to start again fresh, unprejudiced and never smug. When insult is in the air, then you've got to be anchored in wisdom so safely that you can think deeply and surface with a solution that nourishes the enemy as well as yourself. Enemies are those with hunger.

## SURRENDER

Surrender is never looking back. Though what's behind is familiar and beckoning, and what's in front is at best only a dream, surrender is unbroken steps forward. And each step not blundering and determined, but carefully placed and happy. ❧ The first step in surrender is to put your foot on a path, to renounce finally the comfort of the crossroads and opt for a direction. Whatever it may be, the spirit has made a decision. That one step forms the imprint of all that follows. ❧ After that come all the intricacies and joys of travelling, the stringency, the economy, the patience, the humour, the companionship. This surrender is remaining always creative. At every second to contribute virtue to the journey -- not just to make the best of things, but to make them beautiful. There are enemies, of course, but you have to surrender to them too. See their strengths, see their virtues and they die. And if there is no virtue, to be quiet and move on is surrender. ❧ The final stage in surrender is flight. Thoughts lifted away completely from the support of relationship, thoughts filled with so much truth that they naturally lift upwards. When thoughts are this clear, the means of travel changes. From chugging gently along in the company, humouring difficulties, supporting, being supported, there's a departure upwards. This is surrender to newness, to a totally different medium of expression, to a point of solitude, but from where the most subtle companionship and assistance can be given. The highest surrender is to become an angel.

## SWEETNESS

Sweetness is mastery of the senses. Eyes that see to the back of things, ears that hear to the heart of things, lips that speak only the essence of things. Sweetness is the result of a long journey inward to the core of life and the ability to rest there and watch. ☯ Sweetness is living on the line of truth, where you see what is really happening away from the show of words. It is a delicate thing, connected with death, for before dying, it is only that line you see, not the life. Suddenly you understand the why and the what and afterwards you move on. To be alive and happy and yet on this point of death from which you only see what is important is very special. ☯ Sweetness looks for the good in things for at its heart is the conviction that good is somewhere there in everything, if only you have the patience to discover it. False sweetness is saying that something is good when you haven't taken time to find out what it really is and so have lazily hit on something obvious to comment on. Real sweetness feeds only on reality. ☯ Sweetness is the virtue of the very young who have not lost their optimism and sometimes of the very old, in whose contracting lives every moment is worth a lot and whose past has become a hand-picked list of memories which time cannot take from them. ☯ What is really sweet can never be time's victim for sweetness is the quality of a person whose life has touched eternity.

# Tirelessness

Tirelessness is never being washed out; never allowing anything to take away the colour, the vividness, the variations, the beauty of life. And more than anything, tirelessness means never to kill love. As such it has little to do with the body. A smile can build a new foundation, where bricks heaved may just fall or build a place in which people cry. Tirelessness has to do with the spirit. ☯ Tirelessness is when you can stand still in a particular mental position and give whatever you're doing the undiluted strength of that stillness, whether it be the brightness of laughter or the quietness of watching. Whatever the colour, you add that, utter and unmuddied, to the scene. It is then moving from that colour to the next with no hesitation, no blurred edges, suddenly switching according to the need. Tirelessness needs confidence. It also needs love of life to such an extent that there is not even a flinching about the past or a yearning for the future. Now is beautiful and worth mustering energy for. Everything is important. ☯ Sometimes tirelessness is helped by gently withdrawing from the visible scene and focusing on the mental scene. A scene without colour or depth isn't worth concentrating on, but beyond it, someone is calling; there's a job to be done in silence. When you learn to hear distant needs, then you no longer get tired by obvious life. Your mind always finds relevance ... somewhere, quietly. ❧ Tirelessness comes to those with an awareness of time, to those who recognise how critical life is, how each moment offers something much more significant than what is apparent and how, too, there is so much sorrow. It stops you sleeping completely. To develop an awareness of life beyond that of your immediate surroundings brings a healthy restlessness which, used in the right way, infused with peace, is a contribution towards change -- not seen any more than the bricks of a foundation are seen but important. For this tirelessness that feels the importance of things not directly calling you, issues bigger than yourself, there needs to be power. Power comes from reaching upwards, beyond the immediate, and catching a wider glimpse of life, from above. Then resting in that above position: above now, above barriers, above relationships, above the senses, above even your own body. You've left behind the confusion and narrowness that makes you tired.

# TOLERANCE

𝒯olerance is bouncing back even when you are thrown against a very hard wall. A square can't bounce because it is made of straight lines but a ball can because it is round and usually light. Whatever its size, it will just bounce back. To work in straight lines means to miss the implications of things, to be narrow and dictated to by the present. This life is all there is and so you may as well aim for your goals directly. And the corners of the square, the sudden changes of direction, can hurt people. One doesn't associate a ball with hurting, but with playing a game. ☯ Tolerance comes from sensing everything is a riddle and that all things work in cycles, that what is uncomfortable now will soon change. There is constant movement in tolerance, flexibility, because of being content with change. A square finds its position and that's it. Someone who is tolerant can be put in the pocket of any situation, can introduce an element of fun and humour. Humour comes from many things: from a need to cope with inadequacy or hurt, or despair, but the humour of tolerance comes from complete optimism. ☯ How is it possible to have tolerance in a splendid way, as a virtue rather than a necessity? First one has to love quiet, and over and over again make the silent journey inside, watch the picture of birth after birth unfold, mentally to play with that cycle (or ball) of events. This brings such a sense of beauty in you that, though ugliness and problems are seen, they are rightfully incorporated into the design. They give the contrast. ☯ After that, one has to love people, not at all in a superficial way, but as beings who have an intricate design of experiences inside, also as beings who have in their hearts unique talents which are most of the time concealed. When you start to look into people's eyes and see their rarity, and you meet them with your rarity too, then tolerance becomes easy. It is an expression of your respect for quality, for keeping life outstanding. Where there is no tolerance, everything becomes ordinary, which is a shame. It's like standing on the edge of things and scowling. Tolerance is saying yes to the game and enjoying it.

# TRUTHFULNESS

Truthfulness is seeing everything as it is, not from the midst of it, but from the point of its completion. Honesty is seeing things on the way, facing the challenges as they come. Truthfulness is always an expression of optimism because the brush strokes can be sharp. Where there isn't the precision brought by honesty, there is no quality in the picture. In fact, someone not prepared to face the small things will never be entitled to see the whole picture anyway. ☯ In life, a truthful person knows that they should never judge, unless they have understood the secret of time, unless they have seen how change works and how nothing is fixed until the end. A truthful person senses stillness, completion in the distance, but never stills the journey towards it, never lives as though they have reached it, but has it with them always. ☯ A truthful life is one without distraction or delay. Things that glitter do not even turn the eye. There is steadiness, deftness, economy and yet humour because humour comes from the contrast between what the picture is and what it will be. That all being said, truth itself is a gift that is dropped in your lap -- a very deep private thing. It is knowing the whole span of your journey through time.

And that knowing comes only to those who are open. When there is openness with people, warmth, love and trust between you, then in the silences between words, the picture is filled in. Areas of vagueness become suddenly clear and very vivid. Where there is any deception or dishonesty in a relationship, nothing can be added to the picture. You are stuck with the surface of life. Honesty among friends is an opening for God.

## WISDOM

*W*isdom is knowledge of danger but no fear. It is the ability to spot a twist in the path in the distance, a narrow stretch, the possibility of a collision; to stop and wait in peace until something has passed. No wisdom is keeping going, hoping it will all be all right. ❧ Wisdom is also richness, not suspicion or reserve. The richness of experience folded inside you. Experience not only of the past but also of the future, gently knowing what is to come. It is like an income, the interest of which is used daily to live with ease, to avoid pitfalls, but the bulk of which remains saved inside, emerging unbidden when there's a "crater" in your life. ❧ Though there is richness, wisdom avoids show, understands economy and knows that no-one needs your judgement, only your love for life, your warmth and perception. Wisdom simply sees the need and provides, fits in, but remains unique, quietly. ❧ As such, wisdom is not so much a creative quality as one of nurturing what has already been made, what is already there; using what you have to the last inch, squeezing blood out of a stone, because the last drops are worth it. It is seeing the drabness of life and making it beautiful, like a child thrilled

over a button that an adult would throw away because it isn't part of a set.
☯ So wisdom is making the very best of what you have, working vertically not horizontally, not stretching your hand out for more, nor taking on too much. Never saying you will do something, just doing it, not being too enthusiastic, but smiling in the eyes and turning to the task. ☯ It is recognising that every gesture of giving is a right gesture and every gesture of taking is an invitation to influence because, even if you take what you most want, there may be mud stuck to it: the mud of "This is mine" -- heaviness. By giving, as you withdraw, you bring back lightness, it feels right. ☯ And this is what wisdom does. It recognises the rightness of life. It bans protest and demonstration but never strength. It is a life of quiet victories and smiling defeats.

Also by Anthea Church, published by Eternity Ink:

## THE SOURCE

If you delight in the paradoxes so often thrust upon the path to spiritual awareness, you will welcome the thoughts and imagery presented in *The Source*. Anthea Church offers her explorations of relationship with God in meditative prose coloured by everyday experience. The book is an easy to carry size and features 64 individually designed pages printed in two colours throughout. A beautiful gift for spiritually inclined people.

## INNER SPACE

The author's words speak sensitively and openly of her path to a new awareness of being, including both her own experiences and those of her special companions on the journey. We are presented with the challenge to find our own inner space and, through the exploration of this new terrain, to create for ourselves a more peaceful and meaningful existence.

## ANGELS

Across the world, people recognise the presence of divine beings and celebrate their subtle interactions with those who inhabit this physical world. The existence of angels has been a source of fascination, comfort and delight. Anthea takes a closer look at the essential qualities and attributes of an angel — their thoughts, feelings and form — reflecting God's powers.

www.eternityink.com.au

Other ETERNITY INK meditation books, guided meditations and meditation resources are available.
For all resources go to:
www.eternityink.com.au

ETERNITY INK

181 First Avenue, Five Dock. NSW 2046. Australia
Email: info@eternityink.com.au

ETERNITY INK is a publisher for the Brahma Kumaris World Spiritual University. The Brahma Kumaris have meditation centres in over 110 countries. If you wish to find out about the free meditation courses offered and a centre location close to you, please see the following websites:

AUSTRALIA
www.brahmakumaris.org.au

WORLDWIDE
www.brahmakumaris.org

www.ingramcontent.com/pod-product-compliance
Lightning Source LLC
Chambersburg PA
CBHW062115290426
44110CB00023B/2821